SoRting out

GOALS

DEDICATION

Dedicated to the memory of my friend and mentor
Sean Barry. Lovely people do make a difference.

SoRting out
GOALS

GRANT BRECHT

PRENTICE HALL

Sydney   New York   Toronto   Mexico   New Delhi
London   Tokyo   Singapore   Rio de Janeiro

Acquisitions Editor: Kaylie Smith
Production Editor: Elizabeth Thomas
Copy Editor: Loretta Barnard
Cover design: Eilish Bouchier
Ilustrations: David Egan

Typeset by DOCUPRO, Lane Cove, NSW

Printed in Australia by Australian Print Group,
  Maryborough, Victoria

1 2 3 4 5 00 99 98 97 96

ISBN 0 7248 1108 7

National Library of Australia
Cataloguing-in-Publication Data

Brecht, Grant Phillip
  Sorting out goals

  Bibliography
  Includes index
  ISBN 0 7248 1108 7

  1. Goal (Psychology). 2. Achievement motivation.
  3. Self-actualization (Psychology). I. Title.
  (Series: Sorting out life series).

158.1

Prentice Hall of Australia Pty Ltd, *Sydney*
Prentice Hall, Inc., Englewood Cliffs, New Jersey
Prentice Hall Canada, Inc., *Toronto*
Prentice Hall Hispanoamericana, SA, *Mexico*
Prentice Hall of India Private Ltd, *New Delhi*
Prentice Hall International, Inc., *London*
Prentice Hall of Japan, Inc., *Tokyo*
Prentice Hall of Southeast Asia Pty Ltd, *Singapore*
Editora Prentice Hall do Brasil Ltda, *Rio de Janeiro*

 PRENTICE HALL

A Division of Simon & Schuster

CONTENTS

Preface   vi
Acknowledgments   viii
About the author   ix
About the series   x

1   Setting goals — why bother?   1
2   Barriers to achieving goals   6
3   Common goals and strange pursuits   13
4   Balancing a lifestyle   21
5   How to set goals   26
6   Achieving your goals   34
7   How to achieve even more   46
8   Beware of the perfectionist trap   57
9   You know you're successful when . . .   63
10 Living with a goal-less person   69
11 Memory joggers — personal action plan   76
12 Sources of assistance   80

Further reading   83
Index   84

PREFACE

Someone once described life without goals or purpose like a ship without a rudder. A fairly accurate analogy! The best of ability and effort can be wasted if we do not channel it effectively. Effectively means that we do the *right things right*. This is a different state of affairs to being efficient, where we just do things right. Our efforts need to reap maximum reward through the pursuit of meaningful endeavours in our lives.

To be effective in life, and to do the right things right, we need to have a clear picture of those important aspects of life that we value. We can then set goals that incorporate those values and enhance our overall quality of life. This requires planning and a process to guide us along the way. Tracking our goals is also very important to ensure we remain focused and that our short-term goals are stepping stones towards our longer-term goals.

This book will be of great assistance in working out meaningful goals for you to pursue, show you how to achieve them and know when you have been successful. Sources of further assistance are included, and also advice on living with a 'goalless' person.

Setting and achieving goals requires a commitment and some effort on the part of each of us if we are to be successful. The rewards are immense. An enhanced lifestyle, more of the things we desire in life and a stimulating and challenging approach to life.

When we set goals, plan, and achieve them, we become successful—nothing succeeds like success. We remain motivated and confident to go on to other new challenges and discoveries in our lives.

This book in the Sorting Out series will undoubtedly enhance your quality of life and equip you with the necessary insights and knowledge to become a far more effective master or mistress of your own destiny.

Please read, learn and enjoy.

Grant Brecht

ACKNOWLEDGMENTS

My sincere gratitude to all who have been encouraging and of assistance in the endeavour to produce this series of books. My appreciation to the many psychologists from whom I have drawn both knowledge and inspiration. Thank you to Kaylie Smith from Prentice Hall for your guidance and enthusiasm for the overall project. Special thanks to Dr John Lang for his assistance in my final realisation that with a desire, focus and "stick-ability", anything in life is truly possible.

Thanks to Lyn and Oliver for ongoing support and tolerance of my efforts to accomplish a goal. Will I ever forget the words of one gorgeous five year old boy: 'You're not working on those books again are you Daddy?'

ABOUT THE AUTHOR

Grant Brecht is a Clinical Psychologist who works and lives in Sydney, Australia. He is a sought-after presenter and speaker who is well known for his radio and television appearances assisting people to sort out their lives.

Grant is the Director of CORPsych—a psychological consultancy providing employee assistance programs, counselling and training services to companies and individuals across Australia and New Zealand. He has a unique ability to impart information and assist people to learn psychological self-help techniques in a very practical and enjoyable manner.

Look for other books by Grant Brecht in the *Sorting Out* series.

ABOUT THE SERIES

A wise person once remarked that 'Life is not about having no problems, but rather about being able to resolve them quickly when they occur'.

The *Sorting Out* series of books has been written to assist each of us to do just that — to sort out those everyday life challenges that confront every one of us. Whether it be ongoing and unnecessary worry and anxiety, an inability to plan and set goals in life, low self-esteem and a poor self-image or too many perceived demands with too few coping strategies, the books in this series will be of immense practical value and benefit.

Our modern lifestyles are demanding and the rapid rate of social and technological change is placing unprecedented pressures on all of us. Quality of life is determined by how well we predict and rise to the challenges which are placed before us on our journey through life. Our ability to communicate effectively is paramount. Effective communication is about remaining flexible, adaptable, rational, positive and solution-oriented, no matter what is happening in our lives.

This very practical and relevant series of books will assist everyone in developing awareness of the issues and topics covered: how we know if it is a problem for us, including the signs and symptoms, and what we can do about it; how we know when we are successful and where to seek further assistance if we need to; and how to live with someone with a particular concern or problem.

The techniques and self-help procedures in the series are drawn from the latest research into the most effective approaches for dealing with the problems and hassles of everyday living.

CHAPTER 1

Setting goals — why bother?

Good question — why bother? Isn't it easier to put your feet up, turn on the television and veg out? I mean, it is isn't it? Let's face it, if you don't set goals for yourself, you can't fail to achieve them. Yes, I knew there was some reason for it — still one day I'm *gonna* do some of those things I've been talking about, you just wait and see!

It's probably true to say we have all been into that syndrome, so the next question is *are we still there?* Horrifying as that thought might be, it's time to face the facts — are we into the *gonna* syndrome? We certainly can become very apt at making excuses for why we may not be achieving very well in life, or in fact why some others may be. There is always the tall poppy syndrome to fall back on if we get stuck for excuses. That's the syndrome where we try to discredit those who have achieved things we would like to achieve. We often attribute their success to things other than themselves, such as:

◆ their parents are wealthy;

◆ they have always been lucky;

◆ they know people in high places;

◆ they step on others to achieve success.

These excuses make us feel better, and distract us from the reality that we probably have not put in the effort that they have, that perhaps we were not as consistent, well planned and focused on attaining our goals as the achievers were.

So, while some people become defensive and make excuses for themselves, others are enjoying the fruits of their labour. They believe in themselves — 'I do achieve in life, and if it is to be, it is up to me'. By formulating a life script such as this, coupled with well-directed energies, you, too, can be an achiever. Later in the book we will look at writing a life script. The picture is pretty clear, however, that there are those of us who do, and who will, and there are others of us who don't, and who won't.

WHICH CATEGORY DO YOU FIT INTO, AND ARE YOU HAPPY WITH IT?

If you feel you fit into the *don't* and *won't* category, this book is for you. Don't just read it: make sure you then get out there and do it! With the assistance of the techniques and ideas presented in this book, you can gently move yourself into the category of *I do* and *I will*! There are so many opportunities and so many novel and fulfilling pursuits to enjoy.

Now let's have a more in-depth look at why we ought to set goals.

REASON NO. 1 GOALS GIVE US A PURPOSE IN LIFE

You have no doubt heard about the 'What's it all about Alfie?' syndrome. This seldom happens to people who set goals in life. They know what it is all about — it's about doing their best to achieve those goals for their own benefit and the benefit of others. It really doesn't matter what the goals are, as long as they are meaningful to them.

REASON NO. 2 GOALS ACT AS SIGNPOSTS DURING OUR LIFE

How do we know that we are on the right track during our life, that we are actually doing the things that we want to, and are giving those things our best shot? By achieving small goals along the way, we know we are heading towards achieving some of our larger or perhaps more important goals. Retirement is a good example. As we achieve certain investments, levels of superannuation, activities for later life, good health, friends to share life with, we see the signposts that indicate that we are indeed travelling down the right road to our destination — an enjoyable retirement.

REASON NO. 3 GOALS HELP SOLIDIFY OUR SELF-ESTEEM

It's very satisfying when you can pat yourself on the back and say 'Hey, I achieved that, well done'. I hope you know the feeling. If you don't, it means you're probably not setting enough goals for yourself. Setting goals and achieving them can also mean that other people give you a pat on the back in one way or another. It could be a simple 'well done', or it may be a trophy or an award for your achievement, and it may only be an envious glance from someone who is in the *gonna* syndrome. Whatever the payoff, it is all useful fuel to fire up your self-esteem and to remind yourself that you can do it.

3

REASON NO. 4 GOALS INDICATE OUR LEVEL OF MATURITY

The type of goals you set yourself will help you track your maturity through life, or are we setting goals that were appropriate 10 years ago? If we are not advancing our levels of goals, perhaps we are trapped in a particular era of our life and need to set more advanced goals that require a little risk-taking to break out of a restrictive comfort zone. It may be that we are indeed stagnating in life and need to inject some novelty, adventure or learning into our lifestyle.

REASON NO. 5 GOALS HELP YOU ACHIEVE A BALANCE IN YOUR LIFE

Because you are able to set goals across a whole range of life pursuits, they help you to balance your life and get fulfilment from many different areas. You can set goals across the broad spectrum of your life including your vocational, intimate, social, leisure and recreational pursuits. People who set and achieve goals across these areas generally report more enjoyment and meaning in their lives. There is far less likelihood of experiencing a mid-life crisis and there is less likelihood of experiencing the 'what's it all about Alfie?' syndrome. It's great to be ambitious in life, however we need to have a range of goals so that we are also ambitious about the balance.

REASON NO. 6 GOALS HELP US COPE WITH CHANGES IN LIFE

Another very positive aspect of having goals in life is that they are controllable and so can be manipulated and changed to suit your circumstances. This is very important, because as we go through life, circumstances change, we experience different events, we change our priorities, and we can set different goals for ourselves depending on what we want out of life at the time. As we get older, we need to alter our goals to remain realistic about our abilities. For example, we may set higher goals in business, but slightly lower ones for sporting achievements. We may be able to earn more money because of increased experience, but we may be a little slower over a 100 metre dash!

We have just seen six good reasons why setting ourselves

goals in life is so important. There are probably no real surprises, just plenty of common sense, and yet so many of us do not do it particularly well. Why is it that many people do not set realistic goals for themselves during their lives? What are the barriers and most common excuses given? What purpose do these sorts of excuses serve, and what can we begin to do about them?

SUMMARY

◆ Beware of the *gonna* syndrome.

◆ Write an 'I do achieve' life script.

◆ Move from the 'I don't' and 'I won't' set goals to the 'I do' and 'I will' set goals attitude.

◆ Remember the six reasons to set goals:

Circle the two most important reasons you need to set goals.

1. Goals give us a purpose in life. _____

2. Goals act as signposts during our lives. _____

3. Goals help solidify our self-esteem. _____

4. Goals indicate our level of maturity. _____

5. Goals help us achieve a balance in our lives. _____

6. Goals help us cope with changes in our lives. _____

CHAPTER 2

Barriers to achieving goals

Setting goals for ourselves in life does make a lot of sense. We set goals, we achieve them, we feel confident, we go on and achieve more goals! It sounds like the way to go? So why do so many of us have difficulty in making it the way to go! Obviously there is no one common reason. Let's now consider the range of common barriers to achieving goals, and we'll begin with the most common barrier of all:

BARRIER 1 FAILURE TO SET GOALS

It reminds me of that classic scene from *Alice in Wonderland*, where Alice, who is lost, asks the white rabbit which way she should go. The rabbit replies by asking Alice where she would like to go and Alice states that she does not care. The rabbit then replies 'Well, it doesn't matter which way you go'. Like Alice, we may find ourselves unsure of where to go, or what to do next. We may have no clear idea of where we are heading.

Before we can achieve in life we need a clear vision of where we are going and how we are going to get there. With the hustle, bustle and pace of living it is easy to get distracted from planning. We can become so involved and focused on 'just getting everything done' that we don't put any time aside to plan those short-term and long-term goals. The results of this can be quite interesting. We may feel we are being *effective*, and getting things done right. However we may not be at all *efficient* and getting the right things done right. We may be doing things that are not really priorities, or things that are not contributing or adding to our own or our family's quality of life. And why? Because we have not spent the small amount of time required to sit down and decide what we would like to achieve that day, and how that fits with the goals we have set for the future. When we do this, we build more purpose into both our present and future life.

BARRIER 2 NEVER LEARNT HOW TO

You may have grown up in a family environment where goals were not set. Life may have gone on from moment to moment, event to event, year to year and people flowed with it. Sometimes in this way, we may let events in life control us rather than us controlling the events in our lives. During our teenage years, for example, we may have associated with friends who also lived a fairly day-to-day existence, enjoying fairly spontaneous fun and little concern for the future. This pattern of behaviour may then have just become a habit which may have followed us in to our adult years! We may be quite unaware that it is a habit, and blindly go on living a fairly goal-less and directionless existence. At other times, we may be acutely aware that we seem to be going nowhere in life and are having trouble finding meaning in what we are doing — probably because we have not been working on or achieving the things we value in life.

BARRIER 3 TRIED AND FAILED

There can be no greater demotivator than failure. When we fail to achieve something in life it can lead to us becoming discouraged and stopping what it was we were trying to achieve. It can apply to setting goals in life. If we have planned certain goals that have been important for us, and for one reason or another not achieved them, then we may have eventually given up on trying to set goals altogether. We may also get into the 'what if?' syndrome. 'What if I don't succeed . . . What if I only get half way there?' The 'what if?' syndrome is responsible for many of us giving up. Of course failure can be a very valuable learning experience if we react to it positively. Thomas Edison, who eventually gave us electricity, wrote 'I have not failed 10,000 times, I have successfully found 10,000 ways which will not work'.

BARRIER 4 LOW SELF-ESTEEM

Low self-esteem is a nasty thing to live with if it persists for any reasonable length of time. It is quite normal for all of us to experience some self-doubts about ourselves at times. As long as these don't persist for too long, no great damage will be done. However if we suffer from chronic, long-term low self-esteem we will also suffer from a lack of confidence. This leads to procrastination about decision-making — going round and round the mulberry bush with the 'should I do this or should I do that?' syndrome. We then tend to procrastinate even more and put off setting goals and making decisions about our life, so we accomplish very little of real meaning and our self-esteem slips even lower.

BARRIER 5 LIFE WILL HAVE NO SPONTANEITY

Some of you reading this book will have been through periods in your life when you felt that setting goals would mean the end of your spontaneity. You may have thought that you would become a rather dull, boring individual not sought after for partying anymore, so you decided against the goal setting.

This is a reasonably common belief that many people hold towards planning and goal setting, but the reverse of the argument is usually true. When we set goals and plan, we not only free up more time to be spontaneous, but we also enjoy that

time more. This is because we have a stronger sense of purpose and accomplishment, and therefore don't see the spontaneous time as being wasteful.

BARRIER 6 WE SIMPLY DON'T WANT TO
Some of us will stubbornly refuse to plan anything or set any goals. Especially of a mid- to long-term nature. And, of course, at the end of the day the decision needs to be ours. As long as we know why we are making a particular decision and that it is not an excuse, but a preferred option we wish to take, then we have every right to do so. Signs that we may be using the 'I don't want to set goals' excuse could be things like quickly becoming defensive if challenged, a sense of not being fulfilled in life and feeling frustrated with ourselves.

BARRIER 7 OTHER PEOPLE'S GOALS
If we are busy doing things that everybody else tells us we should do, and busy pleasing others, we may leave no time for ourselves to plan for and achieve the things that *we* want in life. It can be quite devastating in later life to find that the things you valued in life were put on hold, while you attended to what others valued, or what you thought they might value

in you. In other words, you were doing things to please others, to keep the peace or to try and look okay in their eyes. It's great to do things for other people, and to work with other people to achieve things, but it is also important to set goals which please ourselves.

BARRIER 8 COMFORT ZONE

Many of us get into a way of doing things and going about our lives that we feel comfortable with. This can be very nice, it allows us to relax and feel at ease. However, it can also be quite restricting and stop us learning, maturing and fulfilling ourselves. In other words, setting goals that might be outside our comfort zone, perhaps something we have not done before, becomes a risk-taking activity which may evoke a degree of fear and anxiety within us. Because of the fear or anxiety we experience, we try very hard to stay within that comfort zone where there is no, or very little, fear or anxiety. However, there may also be very little self-growth and excitement in life!

BARRIER 9 POOR PLANNING

It may be that we do set goals and head out in the direction of achieving them, however enthusiasm and 'a bright idea' may get in the way of proper planning and hinder our ability to actually achieve those goals. Enthusiasm and bright ideas or 'spur of the moment' goal setting is great, but only if it is backed up with realistic and practical planning which will assist us in achieving those particular goals. Unfortunately, we often head off in too much of a hurry and ill prepared for the journey ahead. Later chapters in the book will explain how to plan to achieve your goals, step by step.

BARRIER 10 UNREALISTIC GOALS

At times we set goals that are really beyond our reach or beyond our control. While it is good to think big and to extend ourselves, our goals still need to be within the bounds of reality. The problem with setting goals beyond our reach or ability to plan for, is that, as with other barriers, we become quite demotivated and disheartened if we do not achieve them. We then tend to give up. For example, long-term goals are fine, necessary in fact, and quite achievable if we organise a step-by-step approach to them.

BARRIER 11 EXPECTING OTHERS TO ACHIEVE YOUR GOALS FOR YOU

Now this is an interesting situation, and more common than we might imagine. In this situation we expect our supervisor, our wife, husband or kids or perhaps our employer to automatically move us towards our goals. They may be goals such as a promotion, a happy marriage or our children achieving the things we wish we had accomplished in life. In these cases we may feel betrayed and let down if these expectations are not met, even if we have actually contributed very little to them.

BARRIER 12 OTHER PEOPLE TRY TO OBSTRUCT US

In some instances, and for various reasons, people may actually try to stop you achieving your goals. Why? There are many reasons. It may be out of jealousy for what you have already accomplished. It may be a defensive act brought about because of what they have not accomplished. Another reason may be that the particular person sees you as a threat and so tries to sabotage your progress.

This is obviously not the complete list of barriers that can hamper our journey towards those ever elusive goals. However, it is no doubt enough to give you a good feel for what you may be up against. The beauty of the whole picture is that most of the barriers are self-inflicted. You may not yet understand how they are, but you will by the end of the book. The good news is that, because most barriers are self-inflicted, they are under our control. This means we are quite able to reverse the situations if we desire to and learn how to.

SUMMARY

The twelve common barriers to achieving our goals are:

1. Failure to set them
2. Never learnt how to
3. Tried and failed
4. Low self-esteem
5. Life will have no spontaneity
6. We simply don't want to
7. Other people's goals
8. Comfort zone
9. Poor planning
10. Unrealistic goals
11. Expecting others to achieve your goals for you
12. Other people try to obstruct us.

What are four barriers you are aware of yourself?

1. _____

2. _____

3. _____

4. _____

CHAPTER 3

Common goals and strange pursuits

WHAT ARE GOALS?

What an odd question! What does he mean, what are goals? So many people seem to lack understanding of the importance of goals or how to go about setting or achieving them.

When we really get down to it, the question needs to be *what is a purposeful goal?* When the word 'goal' is mentioned from here on, you can take it to mean a purposeful goal. A purposeful goal is one which enhances our quality of life. A goal which is not purposeful is something we may set ourselves or do which contributes very little to our well-being or quality of life. A goal is:

◆ something you wish to achieve in life;

◆ something you wish to do well in life;

◆ something that has very real meaning to you;

◆ something that gives you a purpose in life;

◆ something that allows you to succeed in life;

◆ a challenge;

◆ a plan, a step towards another goal;

◆ something that directs you and your journey through life.

However we try to define or describe a goal, it breaks down into certain components. First, a goal needs to be owned by yourself. In other words it needs to be *personal*. It needs to have most meaning to the 'setter' of the goal. It may be orientated towards helping or assisting others, but it needs to be something you want to do and achieve for whatever reason. A person is not setting a purposeful goal if they are doing something just to please others. A goal needs to meet the criteria referred to earlier, and something done just to please others generally will not meet those criteria.

Secondly, a goal is always orientated towards *achievement*. That is, doing something better than we have done it in the past, or doing it as well as we had envisaged doing it. The definition of achievement is a very personal thing. What is achievement to one may certainly not be to another. Achievement is not always financial or status orientated, it may purely be something that has very real meaning to you. Achievement does not always involve being better at something than others or gaining more than others. It may be doing something that is your personal best effort, having done it better than you have ever done it before.

Thirdly, a goal is always set with the purpose of increasing our overall *quality of life*. This may be achieved through enhancing our self-esteem or self-confidence levels, and it may also mean a few more comforts in our life. Any supposed goal we set which is not orientated at improving the quality of our life is really a useless endeavour.

So, as long as the goals you set in your life meet these criteria they can literally be anything you want them to be. The chapters to follow will help you decide on the most appropriate goals for yourself so that you are not wasting valuable time and effort chasing things which may not add much to your quality of life.

COMMON GOALS

Now let's focus on what the popular things are that people like to achieve, and some of the more uncommon or unusual goals they set. The thing to keep in mind of course, is that just because particular goals or achievements are sought after does not mean that you as an individual need aspire to, or desire the same goals. What goals you set for yourself need to be your decision, taking into account your needs, the needs of others and life's circumstances at the time. We need to consider our values and desires in life and if they are somewhat unusual, so be it. No one can dictate what our goals will be in life, unless we let them. When we are young and dependent or aged and somewhat frail, it may be easier, and sometimes wiser for others to assist in setting our goals. However, as we grow to a stage in life where we need to stand on our own and tackle the challenges life has dealt us, it is important that, wherever possible, we choose what those challenges will be. This means behaving and thinking in an assertive manner, and realising we have rights as others have rights. One of those rights is the right to establish our own goals and then formulate plans to achieve these. We need to remain vigilant and not get too complacent. Other people and particular events in life may tend to distract us from those goals or in some way form barriers to them. An added challenge then is to successfully break down those barriers and continue on our way.

CASE STUDY

Brendon and Judy had been planning to start a family when they were fairly secure and established in a house of their own. They had been renting since their marriage three years ago.

Three months ago, just as the couple was about to make an offer on a house they could afford, and the bank had approved finance for, Judy was retrenched from her job. The loan for the house had been calculated on both incomes, and the bank now withdrew the offer of the loan. Both Judy and Brendon felt devastated at first, until they sat down and considered their options. Last week they moved into a renovated townhouse that was smaller than the original house they desired, but would comfortably accommodate them with one child. They had decided that starting a family and having some real estate of their own was a priority, the size of the property investment could be increased later if they were in a financial position to do so. Both Brendon and Judy were determined that the loss of her job would not remain a barrier to their goals.

How often do you hear people blaming other people or circumstances for their inability to achieve a goal? Those people are in the Victim Trap referred to throughout the books in this series. These individuals need to look at personal and lifestyle changes to move themselves into an ownership mentality, that is, with an attitude that says 'If it's to be, it's up to me'. While you can get advice and assistance from others in life, the wise people will listen to what everybody else has to say, and then make up their own minds. There will be more about how to move into an ownership mentality as the book progresses.

Let's now consider those common goals that people set:

Career — Aspiring to reach great heights within an organisation, earn lots of money, receive acclaim from others.

Self-growth — The desire to learn more about ourselves and the things around us. To learn about and experience new and novel challenges in life in order to gain a sense of fulfilment and purpose in our lives.

Relationships — A common goal for most people is to establish and then maintain meaningful relationships in many different areas of our lives. These could be very intimate and involved, as in marriage, through to more short-term and fleeting, such as friendships on a holiday. It may include the type of involvement we need with others to carry out our jobs successfully, through to the relationship with the bank manager.

Financial — Once again, the majority of people try to achieve some level of financial security during their lives. This may be working towards having enough money in superannuation, shares or property to retire on.

Health — The statistics show us that not enough people set goals in this department of their lives. Some, on the other hand, exercise regularly, control closely their alcohol intake and eat little saturated fat. Others get into other forms of preventative medicine with the goal of remaining in good physical and emotional health.

Travel — Many young people, and indeed people of all ages, aspire to travel to distant and exciting lands and to see new and interesting things. This may involve the need to plan such a trip from saving the money to establishing an itinerary.

Sport — Australia has many wonderful sporting achievements, thanks to many focused and committed individuals, who set out to be the best and achieved those goals. These are people who are not afraid to set goals which test and stretch their abilities and limits.

Retirement — This, once again, is a very common goal, for which people will plan and prepare in many different ways. When you set clear goals on how you will move from one realm of your life into another, and then actually put those plans and ideas into action, you can make what appears to be a monumental step in your life with a fair degree of ease and certainty that it will turn out well.

STRANGE PURSUITS

Now let's consider some of the strange pursuits that people wish to achieve:

Danger and adventure — Skydiving, mountain climbing, bungee jumping, racing cars, jumping motorbikes over cars and movie stunts are all situations which many of us may consider to be quite unnecessary and perhaps downright stupid! And yet there are those who spend a lot of time, energy and, in some instances, money in the pursuit of these passions. They set goals, plan a method of going about achieving those goals and then go for it.

Pleasing others — Some of us will set goals that are designed to please others and may not be entirely, or even close to what we would like to achieve ourselves. We may do this to appear a nice person to others, or because we are worried that others may reject us or not approve of what we are doing. One of the common reasons we do this is to avoid any form of conflict in our lives. The unfortunate end result of all this is that we may get to a point in our lives when we feel that we have wasted much of our time and our life.

Obsessions — This can be a particularly destructive form of goal setting because it involves a very blinkered approach and narrow focus to life. When we become obsessive about things we lose perspective. We will then often ignore sound advice from other people, and blast on irrespective of the consequences to ourselves or others. Many obsessions are really quite irrational. They may seem strange to others. However if they are not destructive to ourselves or others then why not? For example, some people may become quite involved in hobbies which do not require large outlays of money, so families would not be financially disadvantaged by the pursuit of such hobbies.

Alternative lifestyles — When we look around us it is interesting to observe just how differently people live. Some have goals of living in the city, others of having a country lifestyle. A number of people prefer an 'alternative' lifestyle, and live in communes or in a manner which is far removed from the way most of us

18

would choose to live. Who is right? Who is wrong? Of course it is up to individuals to decide how they wish to conduct their lives as long as it does not unduly affect others. We need to be aware of dictating how others 'must' or 'should' live their lives.

Changing careers — The 1990s have seen people questioning their values and making career changes in their working life that more accurately reflect their values and beliefs. Of course many people have been forced to rethink their career goals due to retrenchment or a restructuring within their organisation. Either way, this may be an opportunity to try other things in life, to look around for another way of providing for yourself or your family and to formulate a whole new set of goals in a totally different way of life.

The message that comes through all this is that as long as they are your goals and don't interfere with your own or others' quality of life they are OKAY. As difficult as it may seem at times, we really do need to be assertive about setting our own goals in life and not doing things just to please others.

Whether our goals are very common, part of the mainstream, or a little strange and unusual, it does not really concern anyone other than ourselves. Those intrepid adventurers who do what many of us may consider to be crazy stunts have a right to do so. One of the things that many people probably do not understand is that many of those unusual and apparently dangerous goals that have been set by those people are often very well planned and implemented. So while they may be strange and unusual, they are also achievable.

SUMMARY — QUICK QUIZ

What are the common goals you aspire towards?

Self growth . relationship

_Health _____

_____

_____

_____

Do you have any strange or unusual goals?

_____

_____

_____

Are your goals in line with your values?

_____

_____

_____

_____

CHAPTER 4

Balancing a lifestyle

n the last chapter I mentioned obsessions. Becoming obsessive about anything can lead to a very blinkered approach to life and to us ending up in a martyr syndrome or a Victim Trap. There is no doubt that setting goals that are ambitious are good for us, however the research suggests that we really do need to be *ambitious about the balance in our lives.*

We all have the same amount of time! There is for everyone, 168 hours in every week. And yet one of the most common excuses used for why we are not doing things that we want to in life is that 'I don't have time'. Crazy isn't it? It's not as if some people actually have 200 hours in their week and that's why they get all those things done! Or, that some people only have 100 hours in their week and that's why they don't get much achieved at all! Every time you multiply seven (days in the week) by 24 (hours in the day) you get 168. We all have the same amount of time, it is just that some of us have trouble getting that balance right.

Why is all of this important? It goes to the very core of achieving things in our lives, that is, that we need to set goals across a range of dimensions in our lives. We can then indeed become ambitious about the balance in our lives and set our goals accordingly. This is much easier done by some of us than others!

THE BALANCING ACT

So what are the areas of our lives that we need to be aware of when we talk about balance? The four major areas are:

◆ *Vocation* — paid work, raising children or some other form of meaningful pursuit;

◆ *Intimate* — family, spouse, partner, children or other very close relationships;

◆ *Social* — friends, community, support groups or similar; and

◆ *Leisure and recreational* — sports, hobbies, outings, holidays, interests.

It is very important to consider how we are doing regarding balancing our lifestyle. It is rather easy to fall into a martyr syndrome and spend far too much time in one area at the expense of the others. This is a little like 'putting all your eggs in one basket'. If something happens to that basket you may lose all your eggs. It's the same with the balance in our lives.

If we put all our efforts and set goals in just one area, and something happens to that area of our life, we may be left with very little to fall back on in the way of quality of life!

CASE STUDY

Kym, a 38 year old, had worked all his life for the one bank. He had started as a teller and gradually risen through the ranks to become the manager of a small country branch. Kym was a loyal and dedicated employee who worked very long hours and spent a lot of after hours' time on bank matters. Although a keen sportsman when younger, Kym had stopped exercising or following the local sporting scene. He spent most Saturday afternoons at work catching up on things and preparing for the next week. When socialising within the local district he was very aware that he was a representative of the bank and was careful about what he was saying and how he was conducting himself. He would often work back late of an evening, and so did not get to see much of his children. His relationship with his wife had deteriorated as he frequently complained of being too tired to go out. There was little effort to socialise unless of course it was work-related. His work was his life and there were few interests outside. Kym harboured the ambition of one day becoming a regional manager.

Two weeks ago, Kym was retrenched during a major restructuring within the bank. He was devastated. His doctor had prescribed him some anti-depressant medication and was extremely concerned about his state of mind.

The case of Kym is a reminder of just how important it is to work on keeping a very well rounded balance across all those important areas of our lives. When we have that balance, and something happens in one of the areas, it is more likely that

our quality of life will remain quite high. We have the other areas to fall back on and to back us up. The balance tends to act as a *buffer* against things like retrenchment or an unexpected illness. There are meaningful pursuits we can go on with and still gain a sense of joy and fulfilment.

The balance does not come naturally to many of us and we have to plan and work at it if we are to achieve it. Some people do it very well without much thought or effort. That is because they have developed certain habits which keep the balance in their life going. For those of us who have not developed the 'balancing habit', planning and some forethought is necessary. The setting of goals in each of the areas mentioned is critical. We tend to concentrate on that area that we have become most familiar with and then just hop on the merry-go-round setting our goals only in that particular area.

When considering establishing a decent balance, we need to set goals that cater for both quantity and quality of time in each area. It is quite common to hear people talk about the fact that it is quality of time that is important. This is a myth! Not only is the research with children showing that quantity of time with parents is important, but when we do not spend ample amounts of time in one area it is very difficult to achieve quality anyway. We tend to rush holidays, spend part of the holiday working, lavish presents on children or do things with them that we think add up to quality and they think are boring or rather silly. We will also find it difficult to form meaningful relationships in which we can build empathy and understanding with others. Our relationships will tend to be built on rather superficial interactions.

The balance that we put in place in our lives certainly needs to be developed around our values and interests and not dictated by others. However we need to be very aware that we are not making excuses for any lack of balance by becoming defensive. We may try to convince ourselves and others that a lack of balance is what we really desire. Some people do seem to be happy with a very restricted and narrow set of activities in life. This is the exception rather than the rule. It is more likely that these people find social or intimate pursuits uncomfortable because they are unused to them. They then elect to stay away from and avoid the situations. They would generally have a far higher quality of life if they desensitised themselves, that is, got used to the situations by facing their anxiety, and then setting goals in their life which included achieving things in those areas.

In Chapter 5, *How to Set Goals*, there will be a chance to consider how the balance in your life is looking across 10 important dimensions which have a marked effect on your quality of life. By considering how well you are doing in those aspects of your life, you will have an opportunity to increase your own awareness of this important issue of balance and set some goals to assist in balancing and enhancing your lifestyle.

SUMMARY

◆ We need to be ambitious about the balance in our lives.

◆ Quantity and quality of time is important.

◆ The four major areas to balance are:
— vocation;
— intimate;
— social;
— leisure and recreation.

25

CHAPTER 5

How to set goals

The information in this chapter is vital if we are to learn to manage our time through life. It is no good setting just any goal, or in fact achieving just any goal. While this may give you some sense of achievement and motivate you to move onto other goals, it may also land you in that fairly heavy 'what's it all about Alfie?' syndrome. What can happen of course is that we may be setting and achieving goals that in the long run really don't mean very much to us! So there is more to setting goals than just picking something to do and then going for it.

The way to understand what I am getting at here is to consider the concepts of *effectiveness* and *efficiency* and to understand the difference between the two.

The differences, as I see them, are:

Effectiveness refers to doing things right, achieving something, doing it well.

Efficiency refers to doing the right things right.

As you can see there is a subtle but very important difference between the two ways of doing things. When you are *effective* you achieve whatever goals you have set. When you are *efficient* you achieve those goals that are very important to your present and future quality of life. So being effective means you get things done, however they may not be important or real priorities in terms of what you would like to achieve in life. To manage our time well and not waste time, we obviously need to be efficient and set goals which are in line with our values allowing us to do the right things *right*.

CASE STUDY

Vicki, a 32 year old mother of two young children, worked part-time as a clerical assistant as well as caring for the children. Vicki spent all day Saturday doing the shopping and running the children to sport. Sunday was spent cleaning and tidying the house. No doubt about it, Vicki had an immaculate house and very contented children — she was doing what she was doing very well. However, Vicki felt bored, fed up and trapped. What was she doing for herself? Where was the fun in life? What enjoyable things did the family do together? What was her lifestyle really all about?

If you see some of yourself in Vicki, you are not alone.

SMART GOALS

If you want to be effective and not just efficient in terms of setting and achieving goals, you need to set *smart goals*, that is, goals which are:

- ◆ Specific: you are able to describe exactly what you want to achieve.

- ◆ Measurable: you will know when you have achieved it and can monitor the steps along the way.

- ◆ Attributable: you own the goal, it is something you want to achieve and will. You have an attitude which says 'If it's to be, it's up to me'.

- ◆ Realistic: make sure it is possible to do, no unrealistic 'pipe dreams', these will only demotivate.

- ◆ Time limit: when do you want to achieve your goal by? Set a date.

The message coming across, of course, is to plan the achievement of your goals. Knee jerk reactions or half-baked ideas are far less likely to work. The likelihood then is that you will become demotivated and fall into the 'why bother?' syndrome, 'nothing ever works out, may as well give up'. The old saying 'success breeds success' is quite true. Small successes one step after the other can add up to very major goals being achieved at the end of the day.

WHAT GOALS?

Good question! It is all very well setting *smart* goals, but how do you decide what it is you wish to achieve? You know they need to be efficient and smart, but what are the goals?

What is important to you? Let's consider the big picture of your life, and what your quality of life is all about.

The goals you set need to enhance and contribute to your overall quality of life. A psychologist, Michael Frisch, has done a great deal of research in this area, and lists 16 things that contribute to or detract from your quality of life. Michael Frisch indicates that you need to consider each of the areas in terms of how *important* it is to you and how *satisfied* you are with that part of your life.

The following activity will allow you to get an accurate picture of your overall quality of life. It will then allow you to select some goals, based on those areas of your life where you are:

(a) not satisfied and wish to improve; and/or

(b) satisfied with but wish to enhance or become even more satisfied with.

This way your goals will at least start off efficient because you will be doing the right things. The next chapter will assist you in doing the right things *right,* which is the next step.

ACTIVITY

Rate each of the following areas of your life specifying what it means to you and how well you are doing in that area.

Meaning to me
1. Nothing
2. Very little
3. Some
4. Fair bit
5. Means a lot

How am I doing?
1. Poorly
2. Just okay
3. Reasonably okay
4. Very well
5. Fantastic

Area of Life	Meaning to me	×	How am I doing?	Total Score
1. Health — I am fit, feeling in good shape.	5 5	×	4 3	
2. Self-image — I like myself and respect myself.	5 5	×	3 4	
3. Finances — I have enough money for my needs.	5 5	×	5 3	
4. Work — I enjoy going to my work and see it as meaningful.	5 5	×	5 3	
5. Relaxation.	5 5	×	4 3	
6. Self-growth — I keep up with things and improve my knowledge and understanding.	5 5	×	5 4	
7. Intimacy — I have close loving relationships which are fulfilling.	5 5	×	4 4	
8. Family — My family is a source of joy, pleasure and fulfilment.	5 5	×	3 3	

9. Community — I enjoy and participate in enough local activities.   _33_ × _32_ ____

10. Social — I have enough close friends with whom I share pleasant times.   _55_ × _22_ ____

To get a total score for each area of your life, just multiply the two scores together and mark in the total score. Then transfer your total scores to the diagram below to obtain an overall profile on how you are going.

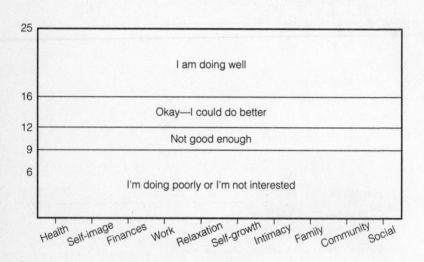

The rest of the activity is fairly straightforward from here on. Select up to three areas that you rate as important to you and that you would like to do better in and note those down. Then select a *specific* goal (the S of *smart* goals) that you would like to set yourself in that area of your life. An example may look like this:

The area of my life is: My specific goal is:

1. Health   To exercise three times a week by brisk walking, so that I **am** puffing with my heart rate at **about** 130 beats per minute.

Now it's your turn to select three actual goals you would like to achieve!

The area of my life is: My specific goal in each is:

1. _____ _____
2. _____ _____
3. _____ _____

Okay, you now need to make sure that you are setting *smart* goals. Completing the following exercise for each goal you have set will allow you to do that. Here is an example.

Goal 1

◆ **Specific:**   To exercise three times a week by brisk walking so that I am puffing with my heart rate at about 130 beats per minute.

◆ **Measurable:** Chart on the fridge to record day's walk. Take my pulse after five minutes to check my heart rate.

◆ **Attributable:** This is important to my well-being. I will make time available and do it.

◆ **Realistic:**   Yes. It's only three hours a week out of 168 hours I have. There are no barriers to me walking briskly. I will start regularly, but build the pace up as I go.

◆ **Time limit:** Start walking three times a week as from next week. Keep it up as a lifestyle habit forever. First goal is to go one month without a missed week.

It's your turn now, so make sure those goals of yours are smart ones!

Goal 1
◆ Specific: S _____
_____
_____

◆ Measurable: M _____
_____
_____

◆ Attributable A _____
_____
_____

◆ Realistic: R _____
_____
_____

◆ Time limit: T _____

Goal 2
As above
S
M
A
R
T

Goal 3
As above
S
M
A
R
T

Well done! Too many of us don't take the time to ensure we plan things well. It comes back to the old saying 'An ounce of prevention is worth a pound of cure'.

Otherwise we can be very haphazard in the way we go about things and not do them properly or very well at all. If this occurs often enough we can develop poor goal setting habits and even end up in that *gonna* syndrome — One day I'm gonna . . .'.

Okay, you have set some goals. The next chapter is all about making sure you achieve them.

SUMMARY

◆ You need to be *efficient* not just *effective*. Do the right things *right*.

◆ Set *smart* goals — Specific, Measurable, Attributable, Realistic and Time limit.

◆ Remember — success breeds success.

◆ Goals need to enhance your quality of life.

◆ Planning is essential — 'An ounce of prevention is worth a pound of cure'.

◆ Beware the *gonna* syndrome.

CHAPTER 6

Achieving your goals

The really exciting part of the whole process is actually getting out there and doing it — achieving those things that are important to your overall quality of life. However, you still have a little more preparation to do before you rush off into the wild blue yonder and set the world on fire.

There are eight basic steps that most successful people follow in achieving goals, even if they are unaware that they are, in fact, following these steps.

The procedure outlined here is important. Try to make it a habit. You may need to practise it a few times, but the time and effort spent will be well worthwhile.

Remember that no great sportsperson, artist, scientist, manager, etc. got to where they are without a lot of preparation, involving *practise*, *practise*, and more *practise*. To stay at the top they will continue to practise on a regular basis. So it is with setting and achieving other goals in any area of our life. We need to practise to become good at it, and then keep practising to stay good at it. There is really only one other alternative open to us if we want to see ourselves as successful and that is to set ourselves goals which are so low and insignificant, that when we compare ourselves with others who are doing or achieving very little in life we may feel we are doing okay. Of course this is a false perception, and will only serve to keep us achieving very little. You are not going to fall into that trap I hear you say, so let's have a look at the eight steps to successful achievement.

STEP 1 SELECT A GOAL

Remember that you selected three goals in the last chapter after considering what your quality of life was all about. One thing that was not touched on earlier was the need for both short-term and long-term goals. Sometimes of course they are built into the one goal. Take exercise for example. Your short-term goal may be to start it and continue it regularly for three months. Your long-term goal may be to make it a habit and continue it for the rest of your life. Other goals may be either short- or long-term. A long-term goal may be to have an overseas holiday in two years' time. If we set only long-term goals, we can suddenly fall into the 'what's it all about Alfie?' syndrome — 'why am I bothering to do this?' It is important that we set our short-term goals as part of the bigger picture of our being efficient in life, that is, doing the right things right. How will what I am doing now help and assist me in the future in terms of improving my quality of life? If you set only long-term goals,

you can become very demotivated because nothing much seems to be happening along the way. You may be unsure if you will achieve the goals because you are not monitoring your progress towards them. In simple terms, you may not have any sign posts to show you that you are on the right road and going in the right direction.

So when setting goals, it is important to consider what you want to achieve in both the short-term and the long-term.

STEP 2 PREPARING TO ACHIEVE

Three things that we are always doing at any one time are behaving, thinking and experiencing emotions or feelings. Once you have set your goals, you then need to *behave*, *think* and *feel* in a way that indicates you are going to achieve those goals.

Behaviour — Make sure your actions are constructive and aimed at achieving. Try not to make excuses, learn new ways of doing things if necessary, and increase your ability levels gradually. Make time and effort available to move towards your goals.

Thinking — Your attitudes and beliefs need to be flexible, adaptable, rational, positive and solution orientated. There is no room for negative, cynical and pessimistic attitudes. Don't waste too much time thinking about what you can't do or haven't done. Spend most of your 'thinking time' considering what you can do, what you have done and how you can build on that. Stop the doubts and uncertainties, and focus on how and why you will achieve the goals.

Emotions — Your feelings can be quite unrealistic and may trick you into believing that because you feel a little uncertain it will be terribly difficult to achieve your goals. Try smiling whenever you are thinking about your goals, and match the smile with positive and optimistic self talk such as 'I can . . . this is a challenge . . . looking forward to this . . .'.

Positive emotions and feelings are generally the product of positive actions and positive attitudes. You need to understand clearly and then practise those actions and attitudes that will assist you in attaining your goals. This positive preparation to achievement is part of what some psychologists refer to as 'positive life scripting'. You write a life script for the way you would like your life to go. It is in fact like writing a script for a play, which you can then act out. So if you write or have a negative life script 'I can't . . . it's hopeless . . . I'll never do it', that tends to be how you will lead your life. With a positive life script 'I can . . . I will . . . you watch me go', there will generally be a quite different scenario — far more positive, useful and goal-orientated.

So the bottom line is that even before you get into the nitty gritty of putting into action what you need to do to achieve your goals, start preparing yourself to be *successful* at it.

STEP 3 POSSIBILITIES AND SOLUTIONS

You have selected a goal or goals, prepared yourself positively and optimistically. Now, how are you going to do it? What are the options? At this stage, make a list of all the possibilities or solutions available to you. Also consider what others may do. Ask for other suggestions if you feel stuck.

SORTING OUT GOALS

For example, say you want to start and then stick to an exercise program that will get you fitter, slimmer and healthier. What are the possibilities or solutions?

1. brisk walking three times a week;
2. swimming three times a week;
3. aerobics three times a week;
4. gym workout twice a week;
5. walk to and from work — 15 minutes each way.

You need to list, or 'brainstorm' all the possibilities you can think of. We will look at how to select a possibility shortly.

Now it's your turn. Below is a chance to list the possibilities and solutions to the goal or goals you have set for yourself.

Possibilities or solutions

Goal 1
1. _____
2. _____
3. _____
4. _____
5. _____
6. _____
7. _____
8. _____

Goal 2
1. _____
2. _____
3. _____
4. _____
5. _____
6. _____
7. _____
8. _____

Goal 3
1. _____
2. _____
3. _____

4. _____
5. _____
6. _____
7. _____
8. _____

STEP 4 EVALUATING THE POSSIBLE SOLUTIONS

You are now in a position to begin working out which is the best thing to do to achieve each goal. To help you make that decision, you need to list the pros and cons of each possibility or solution. Just a few words will suffice and will assist you in your decision-making. Consider the example of the exercise goal.

Goal 1 — begin an exercise program

Possibilities	Pros	Cons
1. Brisk walk	Low cost; easy to do; do it with my wife; low impact.	Not quite vigorous enough.
2. Swim	Tones muscles; overall fitness.	Have to travel to pool.
3. Aerobics	Improve flexibility; meet people; look like a hunk.	Only go at certain times; limited overall fitness benefits; have to travel there.
4. Walk to work	Build exercise into day easily.	Too short — limited benefits; no showers at work.

Now it's your turn. Choose the five most appealing possibilities to work on at this time.

Goal 1

_____

Possibilities or solutions	Pros	Cons
1. _____	_____	_____
2. _____	_____	_____
3. _____	_____	_____
4. _____	_____	_____
5. _____	_____	_____

Goal 2
As above _____

_____

Goal 3
As above _____

_____

STEP 5 SELECTING YOUR PLAN OF ATTACK

For each goal, select the best solution as you see it and then formulate a plan to achieve it.

Remember that your selection or your plan is not set in concrete. If, down the track a little, it becomes clear that another possible solution would have been more appropriate, you can switch across and develop a plan to implement that solution. One of the _barriers_ to setting goals and to generally making decisions about things in life is a _fear of failure_. You can get into the 'what if?' syndrome, where you develop attitudes such as 'what if it doesn't work? what if it's not the right decision?' So what! The attitude needs to be 'that is the decision I made at the time given what I knew. Okay, it hasn't worked so what's the best thing for me to do now?' Then get on and do it! Remember Thomas Edison's words — 'I have not failed 10,000 times, I have successfully found 10,000 ways which do not work'. Let's look again at the exercise example.

Goal 1 — begin an exercise program
Solution selected:　　brisk walking three times a week.
Plan of attack
Starting date:　　Saturday 1 April.
Equipment/materials
　needed:　　Buy walking shoes last Saturday in month.
When:　　Tuesday, Friday and Sunday at 6 a.m.
Who with:　　Myself or with Mary.
Where:　　Five kilometres around the bay.
Other Points:　　1. Build up the pace of walking slowly.
　　2. Check my attitude is positive before,
　　during and after.
My theme:　　I'm important to look after — just do it!

By considering and planning how you will go about things, you are focusing on the fact that this is really going to happen, rather than it being just a 'brainwave' or a good idea that comes and then goes. The example of the plan just given is only a guide, you can put in other points you feel are necessary to achieving your goal.

It's your turn again. Formulate a plan of attack for one or more of your goals.

Plan of attack
Goal 1
Starting date:　　_____
Equipment/materials needed:　　_____
When:　　_____
Who with:　　_____
Where:　　_____
Other points:　　_____
　　_____
My theme　　_____

Goal 2 _____

   As above _____

Goal 3 _____

STEP 6 IMPLEMENTING THE PLAN

By now you should be at the point of just doing it. There are certain things to be aware of that will assist you in getting on with your plan.

First, make sure you put times, appointments and meetings in your dairy. With exercise for example, put the allocated times and days in your dairy or on a chart on the fridge.

Make sure that you plan them into your day or week.

Here is a checklist:

1. Diary/fridge chart/calendar — note all dates and times down, up to a month ahead.
2. Check your attitude — are you determined to do this? Are your attitudes positive, rational and solution-orientated?
3. Support — have you let others know what you are doing so they can support you?
4. Pat on the back — are you giving yourself a pat on the back for doing this?

To get a positive habit in place, you need to focus on what you want to achieve and do, and then work on a regular basis towards achieving it.

STEP 7 TRACKING YOUR PROGRESS

Initially, say once a week (you can gradually spread this out) allow 15 or 20 minutes to 'track' or check on how you are going. This is vital because:

◆ it allows you to focus on what you have done well — rewarding yourself; and

◆ it allows you to quickly troubleshoot any areas or steps which are not going so well. You can then deal with those issues quickly, before they grow into major demotivators.

Here are some hints for tracking your plan and making sure you are on the right track.

TRACKING YOUR PLAN

1. Collect data — does your diary, fridge chart or calendar show that you are doing what you said you would do?
2. Plan ahead — do you have a definite idea of what you need to do next?
3. Attitude — are you still positive and focused on achieving your goal?
4. What are your wins — what are the things to date that you have done well?
5. Barriers/blocks to progress — are you successfully dealing with any barriers or problems which emerge?
6. Changes — do you need to change or alter anything that you are doing in order to become more effective?

It's your turn once again. Consider how your goal or goals are going by completing the following tracking exercise.

TRACKING YOUR PROGRESS

Goal 1   Comments

Collect data   _____

Plan ahead — next steps   _____

Attitude — focused and positive   _____

Your wins   _____

Barriers to progress   _____

Changes needed   _____

Goal 2
   As Above

Goal 3

STEP 8 RE-EVALUATE YOUR GOALS

Are your goals still *efficient* goals? Do they still fit into the big
picture in terms of adding to your quality of life? Are you doing
the *right* things *right*?

Once you have worked through the first seven steps you will
have a fair idea as to whether this is an efficient goal to have
or not. If you still feel that it is a very important issue, then
continue. If not, you may have to modify your goal or even
change it altogether.

Once again the process you have worked through will ensure
you do not have a 'knee jerk' reaction to the situation and change
your mind, willy nilly jumping from one goal to the other.

ACHIEVING YOUR GOALS

Once you have achieved a particular goal there are two issues
you need to consider. They are:

◆ how do I maintain and keep the benefits of that achievement
  going? and

◆ where to from here? what goal next?

Both these issues will be dealt with in the next chapter.

SUMMARY

◆ Remember the eight steps in achieving goals:

1. Select a goal
2. Preparing to achieve
3. Possibilities and solutions
4. Evaluating the possible solutions
5. Selecting plan of attack
6. Implementing the plan
7. Tracking your progress
8. Re-evaluate your goals.

◆ Achieving your goals:
— Maintaining the benefits.
— What goal next?

Remember that achieving goals requires planning and a positive focus. If you believe in yourself, you will do it!

CHAPTER 7

How to achieve even more

By this point you will have set at least one, possibly three goals for yourself, and will be working on achieving those over a certain period of time. So how can you go on achieving even more in your life, continuing to build upon those quality of life issues for yourself? The two questions posed at this end of the last chapter give us a reasonable clue. First, we need to ensure that we continue the benefits and gains we receive from the goals we have already achieved, or are advancing in. So how do we ensure we maintain the gains and build on them?

MAINTAINING THE GAINS

How often have you heard people use the phrase, 'Oh, it was all an anti-climax'. What do they mean? Often they mean that whatever they achieved turned out to be quite a fizzer. Why does this happen? People achieve great things only to find that it is all a bit of a let down. There are several reasons why this may happen.

1. *Poor planning* — Perhaps the goal was not an *efficient* pursuit for yourself. You achieved what you set out to do only to find it did not mean very much to you. Yes, you may have done well at it, but it was not the right thing and not really linked to your quality of life? What did it all mean? This is why the information in Chapter 5 is so important.

2. *The play down* — We can play down what we have achieved by saying things like 'it was no big deal' or 'anyone could have done that'. When we do this, we take the 'gut' out of achievement and leave it all a bit hollow. It may also occur because we do not wish to be seen as a big deal or big-noting ourselves.

3. *Maintenance and generalisation* — What this means is that we may have failed to maintain the benefits (gains) from what we have done. We have also failed to apply those gains and benefits to other areas of our life. For example we may start to exercise regularly but not lose any weight or feel much better because we still eat too much fatty food and drink too much alcohol. So the self-control and diligence we apply to the exercise is not applied to those other areas of our life. We can then become demoralised and demotivated.

So in terms of getting rid of the anti-climax syndrome the information in Chapter 5 will tackle the poor planning. Concentrating on maintaining the gains will tackle the other two points — play downs and maintenance and generalisation.

To go back to the original point, how do you ensure you maintain the gains you have made and go on achieving even more?

You need to:

◆ Acknowledge your effort — look at what you have done and can do, not at what you haven't done and can't do.

◆ Focus on what it is you want to continue, namely those aspects of your achievement that you feel are important to keep going and build into a positive habit.

Don't forget the:

◆ Building blocks — set new goals which build on what you have already achieved. What is the next step for you?

◆ Practise, practise, practise — don't take things for granted; ensure you practise all those positive things that led you to

47

achieving your goals, that is, the planning, attitudes, reviewing. They are all crucial for ongoing success.

◆ Outside assistance — seek support and assistance to maintain your gains if necessary. Are there things you need that only others can provide?

◆ Overcoming barriers to goals — never give up. By giving up I mean throwing your hands in the air and running screaming off into the night! The 'poor me' syndrome is only allowed for very short periods of time, then we need to focus back on the challenge and resolve whatever is happening. So if there are barriers which you encounter, and of course there will be, look for ways around, under, over or through them. You may need to change things a little, do things differently, get outside assistance, spend a little more time, think about it differently, but there is a way of dealing with it. You may not find the way immediately, but you will if you persevere and remain flexible, adaptable and solution-orientated. 'Stickability' is extremely good for you.

WHERE TO FROM HERE?

This was the second question posed from the previous chapter. What goal next? A high quality of life is certainly related to the sense you have that you are achieving in life, that what you are doing is making a difference, that what you are doing is a meaningful pursuit.

Once you have achieved particular goals there may be a blind rush to set more goals in some area of your life in order to gain more of those particular benefits. However, there comes a time when a sideways move may be a very sensible decision. This is very much a part of having that balance in life mentioned throughout the book. Having achieved a particular goal may be a great opportunity to pursue more goals in an entirely different area of your life. Too many eggs in the one basket can be potentially dangerous.

CASE STUDY

Lauren had gone back to work when her youngest child started grade 5 in primary school. Her goal in doing this was to pay off the house mortgage, and to have enough money put aside to ensure a private school education for both her children. Six years later this was achieved and, as a plus, Lauren also had a supervisor's position at the TAFE. What was her next goal? It could have been a higher position at work but Lauren actually set an entirely different goal. She reduced her hours to three days a week, took golf lessons one day a week and played golf with friends on the other day. Her goal was to get good enough at golf to play in the Wednesday women's competition.

We can all learn a great deal from the example set by Lauren. Goals are set to enhance our quality of life, *not* just to get more of something or to gain more status in a job. If that is really what we want in life, fine. However we need to work through, on a regular basis, the exercise in Chapter 6 where we take some time to make sure we are doing the right things right. Remember the profile you did on yourself which looked at 10 areas of your life, how much meaning each area held for you, and how well you felt you were doing in each?

Revisiting this exercise will ensure that we achieve even more goals of a meaningful nature rather than just blasting on through life and suddenly coming to an almighty halt in a 'what's it all about Alfie?' syndrome.

VISUALISING YOUR GOALS

One way to keep on achieving is to spend a little time using what psychologists call 'visualisation or guided imagery'. This is a very powerful and useful technique used by all top-performing athletes, in all sports, throughout the world. The art of visualising yourself achieving certain goals in life is easier for some people than others. When you try this technique, if you have trouble actually seeing yourself achieving the particular goal you have set, then spend some time just sensing or trying to feel what it would be like. Feel the sense of achievement, the quiet confidence, the sense of well-being that goes with accomplishment in our life.

A VISUALISATION/GUIDED IMAGERY TECHNIQUE

Step 1
Find a nice, quiet and comfortable spot. Loosen any tight clothing. Remove glasses if you wear them. A comfortable chair, couch or bed is fine. When relaxed and comfortable, close your eyes.

Step 2
Take a gentle deep breath and sigh the breath out. As you sigh the breath out, say the word 'relax' to yourself in your mind. This is what psychologists call self-talk. Also, as you sigh that breath out, let all your muscles relax and smile. Repeat this procedure three times.

Step 3
Go back to breathing normally, but continue to say the word

'relax' as you breathe out. Let those muscles continue to unwind and keep the smile on your face. Continue this for several minutes.

Step 4
Now visualise yourself achieving your latest goal. See yourself behaving in a way which indicates success with your goal. For example, if the goal is to exercise regularly, see yourself doing the selected exercise and looking fit, healthy and well with a smile on your face. As you imagine yourself like that, use some positive self-talk such as 'good on you mate, well done. Yes I am proud of me' or anything that reinforces your efforts and gives you a realistic pat on the back. Then, in your mind's eye, just reach out and draw that image inside of you, so that it will remain with you over the next weeks as you go about achieving that goal.

Step 5
Go back to focusing on your breathing again, and for a short time just say the word 'relax' as you breathe out, and continue to let those muscles unwind.

Step 6
Before you open your eyes and get used to the light again, run three or four positive self-talks through your head. Open your eyes, get used to the light and you are ready to get on with the rest of your day.

Athletes who use this technique regularly improve their performance quite markedly. When you use it regularly it will assist you in *achieving even more goals*.

ATTITUDINAL EFFICIENCY
You will find this concept mentioned time and time again in all my books. Why? Because it is crucial to achieving any goal in life and is something many of us do notoriously badly. It never ceases to amaze me that the human race has developed amazing

technologies and yet many of us have still not mastered *attitudinal efficiency*.

What is attitudinal efficiency? We use attitudinal efficiency when, no matter what is happening in our life, our thinking and attitudes are:

◆ flexible

◆ adaptable

◆ rational

◆ positive and

◆ solution-orientated.

It's easy to see why attitudinal efficiency is crucial if we are to set up a lifestyle pattern that is aimed at achieving again and again. Let's look at the words.

◆ Flexible — seeing the big picture, all sides of the story, understanding others' points of view.

◆ Adaptable — being open to doing things differently if they work better.

◆ Rational — keeping things in perspective, no catastrophising or making mountains out of molehills.

◆ Positive — 'I can, I am able to, that worked well, good on me, what can I learn, this is exciting.'

◆ Solution-orientated — what is the best thing to do? I will do it as well as I can.

You can remember to use attitudinal efficiency by the acronym, or first letters of each word — FARPS. Just be a little careful how you say it, but it will help you remember this important concept. Every chance you get or can make, practise being flexible, adaptable, rational, positive and solution-orientated with your thinking. Recall things or people you do not like too much and think about them differently. It puts you in a whole different frame of mind and you start to see things quite differently. We may wake in the morning to find it raining and we almost automatically mumble that it's a terrible day. We turn the car radio on and the announcer is mumbling about it being an awful day. How can a day that allows us to put on our favourite jumper, sit in front of a lovely log fire, assist the vegetation to grow, be an awful day? Because we say it is, and of course it is not. It can be a lovely day like any other day, full of all sorts of wonderful goals to achieve and work on. We need to say it is going to be that way and then work on making it that way.

Attitudes and our beliefs have a major influence on our actions and emotional state. So *attitudinal efficiency* leads to *action efficiency* and *emotional efficiency*. A very effective combination for achieving our goals in life is through the formation of positive habits.

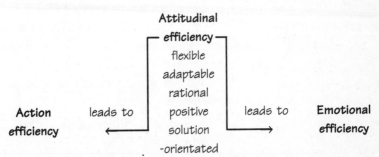

		Attitudinal efficiency		
		flexible		
		adaptable		
		rational		
Action efficiency	leads to ←	positive solution -orientated	leads to →	**Emotional efficiency**

Now it's time to implement some attitudinal efficiency. After reading the case study below, read through the exercise designed to help Jack set positive goals and then try an example of your own.

CASE STUDY

Jack, a 51 year old married accountant with two children, had realised his marriage was in real difficulty when his wife suggested they separate. Jack had worked very hard, with the support of his wife Carol, to build a successful business. Jack realised he and Carol had been under a great deal of pressure during this period. Now, however, he felt betrayed and let down. How dare she opt out on him now, just when they were getting on top of things. Jack felt a mixture of depression, anger and panic over what was happening. He began to lose concentration at work and began drinking heavily to numb his feelings.

Jack's situation is: Carol has stated she wants to separate. Both Jack and Carol have been under a lot of pressure establishing Jack's business.

Jack's attitudes are: This is terrible. She shouldn't do this now. How dare she. What will the future hold? I can't cope with this on top of the other pressures.

Jack can assist himself to cope much better by using attitudinal efficiency. The thoughts and attitudes he needs to have are:

◆ Flexible:
There has been a lot of pressure lately. Carol is obviously feeling it is all too hard.
We have not spent enough time on our relationship.

◆ Adaptable:
We do need to do things differently.
I need to listen to Carol.
I can make changes if I wish to.

◆ Rational:
This is not the end of the world.
It is a major warning sign.
If Carol does go I can build a new life.

◆ Positive: I will give it my best shot to rejuvenate our relationship.

I want the best for both Carol, me, and the children.

◆ Solution-orientated: What are the possible solutions we can implement?

Let's consider all the options.

Do we need some outside assistance to work through this?

I will sit down with Carol and work out an action plan.

Now it's your turn.

A situation I have at the moment is: _____

_____

_____

My attitudes towards it have been: _____

_____

_____

I will assist myself to cope better and set positive goals by using the following attitudinal efficiency (more effective thoughts and beliefs):

Flexible: _____

Adaptable: _____

Rational: _____

Positive: _____

Solution-orientated: _____

You have spent some valuable time looking at developing the right type of attitudes to assist with achieving your goals. Good on you!

SUMMARY

◆ Why achieving your goals can be a fizzer:
  — Poor planning.
  — Playing down your achievements.
  — Failure to maintain or generalise.

◆ Maintain your gains:
  — Acknowledge your effort.
  — Focus on building positive habits.
  — Set building blocks.
  — Use outside assistance if necessary.
  — Overcome the barriers — 'STICKABILITY'.

◆ Don't fall into the trap of setting goals in only one area of your life.

◆ Visualise:
  — See yourself achieving your goals.

◆ Attitudinal efficiency:
  — Having focused thoughts and beliefs will help you achieve your goals. They need to be: flexible, adaptable, rational, positive, and solution-orientated.

CHAPTER 8

Beware of the perfectionist trap

the Perfectionist trap

When setting and achieving goals in life, you need to be very aware of the 'perfectionist trap'. This is where nothing is ever good enough and you keep striving for this intangible thing called 'perfection'. Being perfectionistic refers to a particular style and habit we develop in terms of our attitudes and actions. There is a general feeling that being a perfectionist is good, it means we get things done extremely well and we are very aware about crossing every T and dotting every I. Not so!

Psychologically, having a perfectionistic style can be downright dangerous. Not only do perfectionists tend to stress the hell out of themselves, but they are often stress carriers for others. The classic trait of being perfectionistic is that we focus in on the five per cent we got wrong and forget about the 95 per cent we got right. What's more, we generally tend to do this same thing with others. You can imagine (or if you are one, you already know) the demotivating effect this can have on achieving your own goals or assisting others to achieve theirs. When I refer to a perfectionist style, I don't mean to label the person, or for you to label yourself. I am referring, of course, to the way we approach our behaviour or actions and the attitudes and beliefs that we carry about things.

To ensure that you do not have a perfectionistic style, or that you begin to change your attitudes and behaviours if you do (you'll notice I'm not giving you any choice about this!), I will describe what perfectionistic behaviour is all about. I will then describe the sorts of behaviours and attitudes that are far more constructive. These fall under the headings of *achievement style* and *self-actualisation style*. When we set goals, that we go about fulfilling using achievement and self-actualising actions and attitudes, we are far more successful and less stressed along the way. We are far easier for other people to be around and to work with to achieve those goals. Much of our knowledge in this area comes from the work of Dr Clayton Lafferty and his team of psychologists. They have produced some very valuable research on our 'personal style' (actions and beliefs) and how this affects how successful we will be at achieving goals.

So what are the differences between being *perfectionistic* or *achievement* and *self-actualising* when pursuing goals?

The *perfectionistic* way of doing things is characterised by:

◆ low self-esteem;

◆ excessive demands on yourself and others;

◆ poor judgment due to a preoccupation with detail;

◆ an inability to express or handle emotions; and

◆ excessive worry and fear about making or avoiding mistakes.

Nothing is ever good enough for the perfectionistic person, so they can be quite irritable and impatient when mixing with other people. As mentioned earlier, they are also very demanding of others.

CASE STUDY

Margaret was a 27 year old university tutor. She was also completing a Doctorate in Economics. Recently, an assignment Margaret completed received a Credit rating. All other work from Margaret had earned Distinctions. Margaret was overcome with panic and anger, going between blaming herself and the marker. She told fellow students she was giving her studies up, that she could not cope. Margaret could not get the horror of the result out of her head.

The *achievement* style, which is a very positive way of getting what you want in life, is characterised by:

◆ being as effective as you possibly can in the circumstances;

◆ a commitment to making things better;

◆ setting realistic and attainable goals;

◆ putting effort into what you want to achieve; and

◆ not believing too much in chance or fate.

The *self-actualising* style, that Dr Lafferty and his group has found to be necessary for high achievement, is characterised by:

◆ self-growth and a focus on personal development;

◆ backing up your own 'gut' feeling;

◆ taking responsibility for things without guilt or self-blame;

◆ being challenged and excited about life; and,

◆ involvement and participation in a range of areas of your life.

Both these ways of going about setting and achieving goal after goal in life are very constructive. You can gradually take them on board through practising those actions and attitudes rather than the perfectionistic ones I outlined. Dr Lafferty and his team have researched these issues for many years. The research is backed up by the experiences of psychologists working with a whole range of people wishing to achieve all sorts of different goals.

Now, if you consider that you are a little, or a great deal, too perfectionistic, here are some tips to put into action. They will help you become more achievement and self-actualising in the way you go about your life:

◆ Become aware that your perfectionistic way of doing things can be quite destructive. Make a pact with yourself to work on changing those actions and attitudes slowly. How do you think you got them in the first place?

◆ Lower your expectations and study the results. Was there a disaster? No, of course there wasn't. You may feel a little anxious the first time. It gets easier as you go.

◆ Whenever something happens, focus on the positive aspects first — what went right, what did you do well, what did others do well, what can you learn from it?

◆ Give yourself regular pats on the back for what you can do and what you have done instead of getting all concerned about what you can't do and what you haven't done.

◆ Generally become less demanding on yourself and others.

◆ Practise accepting failure and mistakes in a positive way — the attitude needs to be 'I am allowed to make mistakes and I will learn what I can from them'.

◆ Make sure you keep a good balance in your life with ample time to relax, exercise and get plenty of sleep.

◆ Start now — not tomorrow or the next day, right now! Let's develop a *plan*.

CASE STUDY

Lyn, 43, had taken up jogging two years ago to keep fit. She had started running half marathons to help with her motivation of staying fit and to set personal goals. The goal for the last half marathon was to run it at least five minutes faster than the previous one. She in fact ran in two minutes slower. Lyn was disappointed when she crossed the finishing line. She did not beat herself up, however, she allowed herself to feel disappointed for a while, and then switched her thinking and gave herself a pat on the back for running and finishing. Work and her home life had been busy which meant she had not trained as often as she had for the run before. So, taking everything into account she had run well. Her focus now is the next half marathon in two months' time. Her goal is to finish seven minutes faster than her last run. The finisher's medallion around her neck was a nice reminder that at 43 years of age, she could still run 21 kilometres, which is a great achievement in itself.

YOUR ANTI-PERFECTIONIST PLAN

The perfectionistic behaviours and attitudes I have that I am aware of include:

1. _____
2. _____
3. _____
4. _____
5. _____

I will substitute these with:

1. _____
2. _____
3. _____
4. _____
5. _____

SORTING OUT GOALS

The achievement and self-actualising actions and attitudes I will keep going or develop include:

Achievement

_____

_____

_____

_____

Self-actualising

_____

_____

_____

_____

You need to review these actions and attitudes regularly to ensure that you are on the right track. By taking the time to consider these issues, you are indicating that you are important to look after as a person and so are your goals and aspirations in life.

SUMMARY

◆ Beware of the *perfectionistic trap* where nothing is ever good enough.

◆ A perfectionistic style is made up of personal attitudes and actions which are unrealistic and self-defeating.

◆ A perfectionistic style will make you a stress carrier for other people.

◆ You need to develop *achievement* and *self-actualising* styles rather than a perfectionistic style.

◆ Use positive, rational and solution-orientated attitudes and actions in your *anti-perfectionist plan*.

CHAPTER 9

You know you're successful when . . .

The 50 million dollar question! How do you know when you're successful? It may seem a somewhat trivial thing to ask, but it certainly is not a trivial matter. What happens if we do not know we are successful, or feel that we are not successful but are not really sure? Our self-esteem can take quite a dive, our confidence slump and we may continue to feel things are not right long after they actually are. Frustration, uncertainty and the whole syndrome of 'chasing your tail' can occur. The unfortunate part of all that, of course, is that we miss out on that wonderful feeling that having achieved something can bring, that is, that sense of doing something very well, of being recognised for your expertise and of generally feeling in control of life and your own destiny. It makes all the hard work of settling down and getting into things worthwhile. So what are the signposts that indicate that we are succeeding?

SIGNPOST 1 A PLAN

It may sound a little strange, but the first sign of success is when we plan to be successful. The earlier chapters showed you how to plan what goals you wish to pursue and then how to implement that plan. A key indicator of a successful plan is its ability to help motivate the person who is trying to accomplish that particular goal. Now you might ask 'how does an actual plan motivate?' A plan will assist with motivation to achieve the goal if it has a step by step approach to where you would like to get to, with no unrealistic large leaps you have to take which may see you get out of your depth. A plan will also assist motivation if it asks you to pat yourself on the back for every step you accomplish along the way.

In psychological terms we say you need to:

◆ have a graduated approach to where you are heading, and

◆ you reward yourself for achieving every step in the graduated approach.

Remember not to take yourself or anything you do for granted. Pay yourself off, even if it is only a pat on the back for everything you do well. It helps replenish your *supply of self-esteem*. Let's face it, there are plenty of people and events in life that can undermine that supply and reduce it greatly if you let them. Don't let them! Replenish those supplies frequently.

SIGNPOST 2 A CLEARLY DEFINED GOAL

Once you have achieved that goal which you clearly defined, you are successful. So it is important to know exactly what it is you wish to achieve from the beginning. A goal like 'I want to be successful' is far too unclear. A goal like 'I will exercise three times a week for 3 months' is very clear. At the end of the three months a huge pat on the back and some form of significant reward for yourself for sticking to it is appropriate. Of course you should also have been paying yourself off for the entire three months in terms of looking at what you have been achieving as you go.

So, clearly defined goals will enable you to know when you are successful.

SIGNPOST 3 INTERNAL CONTROL

A feeling that you are in control of yourself and master or mistress of your own destiny is another sure sign that you are achieving in life. When you achieve those goals that you have set for yourself there is a feeling that your quality of life is well within your control and that many things are possible. You tend to look more for the ways that things can be accomplished, and focus far less on the hurdles or barriers that are there.

It is interesting that fate or luck then plays a far smaller part in your life. You find that the words 'I was just lucky' or 'It's all up to chance really' are used far less often. You develop that positive attitude that says 'if it's to be, it's up to me'.

SIGNPOST 4 CHALLENGES

Another sure sign of being successful in accomplishing goals is when we view goals and tasks in life as *challenges* rather than as problems. When we see something as a challenge, the energy flows in and we lean forward and say 'Okay, now how can I resolve that'. When we view things as problems, we sit back, the energy flows out and a large dark cloud surrounds us. We then tend to say things like 'I can't stand it, it's awful', 'How will I ever get over this?', 'It's a catastrophe'. Challenges in life provide us with vitality, energy and a vibrance which can be quite contagious — other people feel it when they are around us. It is not only necessary, it's good for you. You know you are achieving when you have it, and of course success breeds success.

SIGNPOST 5 CHANGE

How we deal with change is another way of gauging how successful we have been at setting goals and achieving them. People who look at the *advantages of changing*, and the *disadvantages of not changing* are generally those who are successful. Those who look at the *disadvantages of changing* and the *advantages of not changing* are more likely to be non-achievers and dependent on others to direct them through life and provide for them. This does not mean that we blindly accept change. However it means we get what we can from it and accept that in many areas of life, if we want to live in the mainstream, change is inevitable.

SIGNPOST 6 RISK-TAKING

Successful people take risks. They are not always huge ones, but successful people certainly back their own judgment and have a go. They tend to realise that everything in life is fallible. There is nothing we can say that will or will not definitely happen, except death. That's pretty certain! Risk-taking is necessary if we are going to have a go at making the most of our life. We need to step out of our *comfort zone* from time to time to experience the bigger picture. If not, we may go on being *effective*, doing things *right*, however we may be far from being *efficient*, that is doing the right things right. Small risks with moderate ones every now and then may be enough for us to feel safe outside of that comfort zone and so enable us to set goals across the balance of our life.

SIGNPOST 7 CONFIDENCE

A very healthy level of self-confidence is perhaps the clearest indicator of being successful. Self-confidence is normally developed from having set goals and achieved them. The more that we repeat this pattern the more self-confidence we tend to have.

Success at achieving things in life replenishes the self-confidence that we may lose when a number of things in a row do not go as planned. We can still keep our confidence up if we work on it, but we may lose little bits from time to time. That's why replenishing it regularly is so useful. Confidence is reflected in the way we act, think and feel. It comes out in all three areas. We can have a lot of self-confidence without becoming big-headed or too conceited.

SIGNPOST 8 ALL AROUND YOU

When people are successful they are surrounded by it. They have in their life what they want to have there — certain types of people, certain possessions and certain types of activities and everyday pursuits. They are not the type who gets envious or defensive, they don't feel the need to. They are already doing what they want to do, and achieving what they want to achieve. Of course life still has its challenges, and sometimes they may be 'stumped' momentarily. That's the secret! Successful people only allow themselves to stand still momentarily, and then they work out a solution and have a go. So if you are wasting too much time procrastinating, going backwards and forwards about what you might do, stop it and get on with a solution. It means you still have a little distance to travel to be successful. That's not necessarily bad news, if you see it as a challenge rather than a problem.

Even if you feel you are not successful at setting and achieving goals at this point in your life, don't despair. All you need to decide is that *you are important*, take note of the techniques described in this book, and *change* the way you do things. Remember that there is no time like right now!

SUMMARY
- ◆ Signposts of success
  - — A plan — you plan to be successful.
  - — A clearly defined goal.
  - — Sense of internal control.
  - — Challenges rather than problems.
  - — Adaptation to change.
  - — Taking risks.
  - — Healthy level of self-confidence.
  - — You are surrounded by it.
- ◆ Remember that there is no time like right now.

CHAPTER 10

Living with a goal-less person

Is your life going around and around in circles, getting nowhere? This is the plight of people who do not set goals in their life, and it can be your plight also, if you live with a person like this and do not remain ever vigilant. As has been stated in other books in this series, if you are living with a 'goal-less' person you need to have a very fixed attitude that *you* are important to look after and you must do just that. One person going nowhere is unfortunate. Two going nowhere makes no sense whatsoever.

How do we know a person is goal-less? If there is nothing they are enthusiastic about in the short- or long-term, then that person is probably goal-less. A desire to get out of life rather than into life through the use of too much alcohol or hard drugs is also a sign of aimlessness. The person who complains that their life is going nowhere and that they are finding it difficult to find meaning in what they are doing is displaying the obvious warning signs.

Someone who has martyred themselves to a particular thing in life such as their work may also have lost sight of the goals across the balance of their life. This person may be just as demanding and difficult to live with.

So what to do?

I'M IMPORTANT

Don't join them on the merry go round — make sure you hop

off. Your attitudes and behaviours need to remain focused on setting and achieving goals for yourself. You can still be concerned for the 'goal-less' person while getting on with your own life. So even if that person will not read this book, you have been sensible in reading it for yourself. Make sure you put into action the techniques and ideas you have been reading about here. Yes, there can be a strange sense of guilt when we are doing okay and someone we are close to is not. Remember, while you are doing okay and your self-esteem is good, you are in a better position to be able to assist the other person. If you are not achieving and feeling badly about yourself, you are probably not likely to be able to help them.

Set goals and achieve them, you owe yourself that.

STOP THE BLAMING!

One of the traps we can get into when we live with this type of person is that they are a useful *scapegoat* for everything that is not going well in our life. We say or think things like 'If only they would get off their backside and . . . : my life would be okay'. It probably wouldn't be. If we don't have the desire to get going just because someone else doesn't, we are unlikely to start taking more control over our life just because they do. In the short-term we may get dragged along with them. Generally it is short-lived and we will find someone or something else to blame for our inactivity.

Indeed it can be handy having someone else to dump on, and that is one reason why some people like to have non-achievers around. It is unfortunate if it gets to this stage; however it certainly can happen.

We need to replace the *blaming* with taking responsibility for ourselves.

No matter what someone else elects to do with their life, we still control ours to a very great extent. We need to have a *vision* of where we want to go, and how we want our life to go, and then set a plan to get there. Others generally only get in the way because we allow them. Don't allow them to.

Another 'blame trap' is to blame ourselves for why someone else is not achieving, so be careful not to fall into this trap. Adults have choices and they need to utilise them. You cannot be totally responsible for another adult. They have options to get help, leave, do things differently and so on. It is up to them to take responsibility for themselves.

THE HELPER ROLE

Trying to assist someone to develop goals and plans for their life if they have none is an absolutely fine thing to do. As long as you remember the points in the last two scenarios you may be in a position to do just that — help someone get their life more in order. How can you help?

EMPATHY

Unfortunately most of us are not very good at understanding other people. We often make judgments too quickly, mind read, make assumptions and jump to conclusions as to where the other person is coming from, which is hardly the way to go about developing an understanding of someone else's situation. Also when we do try and understand someone else, is it because we:

◆ have a need to be needed?;

◆ want to be able to assist them effectively?;

◆ or a mixture of both?

The most common reason, of course, is the 'mixture of both'. If we gain and the other person gains, it's a win-win situation. Most people seem to like that outcome.

We need to understand others so we can appreciate why they are that way, and how they feel about it, and so we can work out what we want to do or what we can help them with.

How do we go about getting that understanding?

1. Develop and practise an attitude that says 'I do want to understand'. Know why you want to understand.
2. Speak to the other person about the situation when you are both calm, not in the middle of an argument about something.
3. When you make a time allow plenty of time to talk.
4. Listen, listen, listen — do not attempt to mind read or jump to conclusions.
5. Clarify anything you do not understand.
6. Acknowledge that you understand the other person is feeling that way.
7. Do not make moral judgments about what is being said.
8. Decide on a plan of action, or make a time to work on one.

ACTION PLAN

Once you understand where the person is coming from, you are ready to go into the action stage with them. Your main aim here is to assist them in developing a plan of action that will result in them gaining control over the aimlessness of their life and to develop more direction and purpose through setting goals. In as practical a manner as possible, assist the person to:

◆ define what is happening — keep it specific;

◆ how do they feel about it?;

◆ what solutions are there — brainstorm;

◆ sort out the solutions — the good and bad points of each;

◆ settle on a solution — choose the most practical one at the time;

◆ work out a plan of attack — how will they go about it;

◆ what support would they like, and are you prepared to give?;

◆ plan to sit down and review progress in a few months' time.

JOINT GOALS

You can also suggest joint goals, things you desire to achieve together. This can be especially rewarding and supportive. It also allows you first hand to show the person how to go about setting and achieving goals.

CHARACTERISTICS OF EFFECTIVE HELPERS

Effective helpers tend to:

◆ be positive and optimistic;

◆ be in control of their own life;

◆ realise they can only help others to help themselves;

◆ use praise at least three times as often as criticism;

◆ not fall into a rescuing role;

◆ know their limitations;

◆ ask for extra assistance if necessary;

◆ keep a good balance in their lives;

- show genuine concern for others;
- not project blame out onto others;
- rely on themselves;
- have a high self-esteem.

A CHECKLIST

1. Do you have a goal-less person living with you?
   Tick Yes . . . No . . . If Yes, go to 2.
2. Have you tried to be empathic? Tick Yes . . . No . . .
3. If you have, why are they goal-less? If No, attempt this with the person.

   _____

   _____

   _____

   _____

4. Have you set an action plan with them? Tick Yes . . . No . . .
5. If Yes, what is it? If No, try and get to this point.

   _____

   _____

   _____

   _____

   _____

6. How are you supporting the person?

   _____

   _____

   _____

7. You're important to look after. How are you looking after yourself?

   _____

   _____

   _____

   _____

   _____

SUMMARY

- ◆ Two people going nowhere makes no sense.
- ◆ You're important to look after.
- ◆ Stop the blaming — others or yourself.
- ◆ The helper role:
    - — empathy;
    - — action plan;
    - — joint goals.
- ◆ 12 characteristics of effective helpers.

CHAPTER 11

Memory joggers — personal action plan

It is now that time when we see if you have been paying attention. It is really an opportunity to make sure you have a good understanding of the important issues and techniques covered in the book. At the same time you will have the opportunity to consider a 'personal action plan' for yourself.

You need to make sure you have a realistic view of the big picture regarding setting and achieving goals in life. The idea with the following exercises is to:

♦ attempt to answer the questions by filling in the spaces;

♦ check your answers by going back to the relevant chapters;

♦ find the answers by going back to the relevant chapters; or

♦ use them as a revision of the book.

1. Why bother to set goals at all?

_____
_____
_____
_____

2. Barriers you see to you achieving your important goals?

_____
_____
_____
_____

3. What is the balance in your lifestyle like? Why?

_____
_____
_____
_____
_____
_____

4. What gaols have you set for yourself?

_____
_____
_____
_____

5. What is your plan to achieve those goals?

_____
_____
_____
_____

6. What are the benefits to you of achieving your goals?

_____
_____
_____
_____

77

7. What happens once you have achieved your goals?

   _____
   _____
   _____
   _____

8. Are perfectionistic behaviours and attitudes a problem for you? If they are, what are they? How can you change them to be more achieving and self-actualising?

   _____
   Perfectionistic: _____
   Achieving and self-actualising: _____
   _____
   _____

9. How will you gauge your success in achieving your goals?

   _____
   _____
   _____
   _____
   _____

10. Is there a goal-less person in your life? If there is, what do you need to start, or continue doing?

   _____
   _____
   _____
   _____
   _____
   _____

11. Why are you important to look after?

   _____
   _____
   _____
   _____
   _____

It's critical to take the time to consider the big picture. Make sure you continue the attitude that 'I am important to look after'.

CHAPTER 12

Sources of assistance

If you feel a little overwhelmed by the road ahead in terms of what you need to do, there are extra sources you can turn to for advice, support or counselling on the topic of setting and achieving efficient goals.

One of the major considerations is *support*. If you have tried something before and not achieved the level you had hoped to, it may seem rather daunting to have another go. In a case like that, it may be necessary to make sure that you have adequate support as you give it your best shot this time. There is much support for goal setting that is available to you.

SPOUSE/PARTNER/FAMILY

These people in your life may be very willing and very able to help you stick to your goals if they know exactly what you would like from them. People are more likely to offer support and assistance if they see that you are giving it your best shot also, and if they can see that you are not becoming dependent on them, but that you require their help so you can better learn to help yourself. Remember to thank them. This helps tremendously.

What about setting mutual goals? Goals that you are both aspiring towards as a couple or as a family unit. The lovely thing about these goals is that they give mutual purpose as well as a sense of achievement to each person.

PSYCHOLOGISTS

Psychologists can also be of further assistance by helping formulate, plan and troubleshoot your goal achievement activities. Psychologists can be found under P in the Yellow Pages.

Ensure that the psychologist is registered in your State, and has experience in assisting people with this type of challenge in life. If the psychologist is in private practice, you will have to pay for the advice or counselling. The costs vary from around $60 per hour session to $145 per session depending on the individual psychologist. The recommended fee per hour consultation laid down by the Australian Psychological Association at the time this book was published was around $140 per hour session.

Psychologists can also be found in community health centres and major hospitals, where their services are generally free.

AT WORK

If you are in paid employment, your manager or supervisor may also be, and hopefully is, a useful support in what you would like to achieve in that environment. It is generally crucial to let your manager or supervisor know what you wish to achieve in the work place so they can assist you in your goal.

This may involve sending you on training courses, or alerting you to particular positions which will be becoming available so you can prepare your resume and make an application. However, they can only do this if they have a very clear understanding of what you want, and what you are achieving where you are. A track record in success is a great introduction to another success. As the saying goes 'nothing succeeds like success'. Your company may also have an Employee Assistance Program in place where you can get free confidential advice and counselling for any personal or work-related problems.

MENTORS

This is where you align yourself with someone who is already doing the sorts of things you would one day like to be doing.

The idea is to watch and learn, taking on board the skills you see that person exhibiting. You need to be able to get yourself into a situation where you can have that person monitor your progress and give you feedback on how you are going. It can be a very rewarding experience, as well as company along the way to achieving your goals.

Remember that you are important to look after so if you need to avail yourself of extra support do it.

Life is too short to hold back, so go out there and achieve those goals. Remember that a mighty journey starts with that one small first step.

Take care, all the very best on your travels through life, and enjoy the journey.

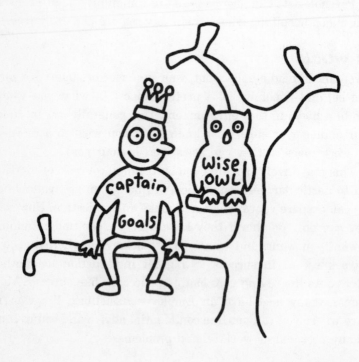

FURTHER READING

Brecht, G. *Sorting out Self-esteem*, Prentice Hall, Sydney, 1996.

Brecht, G. *Sorting out Stress*, Prentice Hall, Sydney, 1996.

Brecht, G. *Sorting out Worry*, Prentice Hall, Sydney, 1996.

Burns, D. *The Feeling Good Handbook*, William Morrow, New York, 1989.

Montgomery, R. *The Truth about Success and Motivation*, Lothian, Melbourne, 1987.

Seligman, M. *What You Can Change and What You Can't: The Complete Guide to Successful Self-improvement*, Random House, Sydney, 1994.

Van Fleet, J. *Power Within*, Prentice Hall, Englewood Cliffs, New Jersey, 1994.

Wilson, S.B. *Goal Setting*, Prentice Hall, Englewood Cliffs, New Jersey, 1993.

INDEX

achievement style, 58–59, 62
achieving goals
    barriers, 6–12
    basic steps, 34–45
    furthering the benefits, 49–55
    maintaining the
        benefits, 46–48
    preparation, 36–37
action plan
    goal-less people, 73
    personal, 76–79
adventurous goals, 18
alternative lifestyles, 18
anti-perfectionist plan, 61
assistance, 48, 80–82,
attitudinal efficiency, 51–55

balance in life, 4, 21–25
barriers to achieving
    goals, 6–12, 15, 40
    overcoming, 48
blaming, 16, 70–71

careers
    balance in life, 22–25
    changing, 19
    evaluating work, 29, 30
    goals, 16
challenges, 65
change
    careers, 19
    coping with, 4, 66
children, 11, 24
comfort zones, 10, 66
common goals, 14–17
community, 29, 30
confidence, 66

dangerous goals, 18

efficiency and effectiveness, 26
emotions, 37
empathy
    helper role, 71–74
evaluation
    possible solutions, 39
    quality of life, 28–33,
    re-evaluating goals, 44

failure, 7, 40, 60
families, 11, 29, 30
    sources of assistance, 80
"farps" attitudes, 52–56
financial goals, 17, 29, 30

goals
    barriers to, 6–12, 48
    clearly defined, 64
    common, 14–17
    how to set, 26–33
    selection, 28, 35–36
    setting, 1–5
    strange pursuits, 18–20,
    success, 63–68
    what are they?, 13
goal-less people
    living with, 69–75
guided imagery technique, 50–51

health, 17, 29, 30
helper role, 71–74

internal control, 65

joint goals
    goal-less people, 73

leisure and recreation
    balance in life, 22

lifestyles
   alternative, 18
   balancing, 4, 21–25

maintaining benefits of
   goals, 46–48
martyr syndrome, 21
maturity, 4
memory joggers
   personal action plan, 76–79
mentors, 81

obsessions, 18, 21

perfectionist trap, 57–62
plans
   anti-perfectionist, 61
   goal-less people, 73
   implementation, 42
   personal action plan, 76–79
   plan of attack, 40–41
   signs of success, 64
   tracking, 43
planning
   poor, 10, 46
   setting goals, 26–33
pleasing others, 9, 18
psychologists, 81
purpose in life, 3

quality of life, 28–33

recreation
   balance in life, 22
relationships, 17
   balance in life, 22–25
   goal-less people, 69–75

sources of assistance, 80
retirement goals, 17
risk-taking, 66

selecting goals, 28, 35–36
self-actualisation style, 58–59, 62
self-confidence, 66
self-esteem, 3, 8
self-growth, 16, 29, 30
self-image, 29, 30
setting goals,
   how, 26–33
   reasons for, 1–5
signs of success, 3, 63–68
"smart" goals, 27–33
social life, 22, 29, 30
sport
   common goals, 17
   unusual, 18
spouses, 11
   sources of assistance, 80
strange pursuits, 18–20
successful goals, 63–68
support, 80–82

time management, 26
travel, 17

unrealistic goals, 10
unusual goals, 18–20

victim trap, 16, 21
visualising goals, 50–51

work–see careers
workplace
   source of assistance, 81